The Complete Composting Guide for Beginners: Grow Your Own From Home!

By

Linda Marsden

Table of Contents

Hello and welcome to *The Complete Composting Guide for Beginners*. Inside, you'll find everything you need to know about organic waste composting. Composting is a vast subject to deal with. Despite the many hours spent in researching and pouring over a variety of resources, a lot of information still awaits to be discovered and further studied.

This book will explore several distinctive and yet integrated parts in an attempt to answer various questions on compost and composting. The first part deals with the combined question, "What is Composting?" Included in this are brief descriptions of twelve different types of composting from ancient times up to the present.

The second part explores ethical and environmental concerns over organic waste addressed by composting and the third answers the question, "What is Home Composting?" This chapter will differentiate casual or traditional composting from gourmet or indoor composting and describes bokashi composting as a fast-track type of anaerobic composting.

The fourth part of this book answers "What Can You Compost?" by a description of the four essential composting ingredients (the greens, the browns, water, air) and other vital components, followed by a handy list of examples of what can and cannot be composted.

The remaining part of this book discusses the "nitty-gritties" of troubleshooting techniques for home composting, how to make one's own compost at home with step-by-step details of two main types of home composting and a variety of ways to use compost. You will also find out about the Health Hazards and Risks of Composting so you will have a good understanding of the ins and outs of composting by the end of this book.

Happy composting!

Linda Marsden

INTRODUCTION

We, homo sapiens, are responsible for the wellness of our Planet Earth. Our attitude towards our environment reveals much of who we are. How can we conserve nature's bounty and preserve the environment even as we pursue economic progress? We don't want to be that irresponsible kid who carelessly neglects to clean up after himself, do we? We see how pollution, global warming and natural disasters devastate wide swathes of our planet. Yet, each individual can initiate a few steps that will impact the environment positively.

Runaway economic growth continues to deplete natural resources that future generations need for survival. Water, abundant and free in some parts of the world, is a precious and dwindling commodity in harsh, inhospitable regions. Thousands eke out a bare existence in desert-like terrain where every drop of water counts and every blade of grass spells life or death to livestock. On the other hand, affluence and over-abundance in wealthy communities result in mountains of garbage.

Every day, tons and tons of refuse and trash are generated, collected and dumped into landfills. We realize that the only sustainable way to go is for everybody to do his bit to "reduce, reuse, and recycle". The problem of waste is the flipside of economic growth. There is concerted effort and renewed interest worldwide to address organic waste disposal. While governments put in place massive composting and other operations to recycle waste by mechanized and commercial methods, there are positive small-scale measures citizens can do to maintain a cleaner and greener planet.

Home composting is one such endeavor. Most of us generate trash on a daily basis. A lot of what we throw into the trash bin is headed directly to a landfill - and landfills are disgusting! Nobody wants to live near a smelly landfill. We can help reduce the volumes of trash sent to the landfills – by composting our organic waste at home. In 1845, Julia Carney wrote: "Little drops of water, little grains of sand, make the mighty ocean and the beauteous land". The little environmental-conscious acts we do as individuals add up to eco-impacting miracles in our world.

Compost is a garden product - it is nutrient-rich organic material that looks much like natural humus (the soil that builds up naturally on forest floors). The decomposed organic matter gives compost its crumbly texture. Compost is a natural alternative to store-bought chemical fertilizers that plants and flowers love. Compost buffers soils that are too alkaline or too acidic.

When you compost food and garden scraps, you are simply recycling them to be used afresh by plants. Compost is a natural fertilizer that is so important to grow those pricey organic vegetables, fruits and flowers we see in the supermarkets. We can improve our garden soil by adding commercially prepared compost which we can readily buy from the shop. Or we can try a hand by making it ourselves. Compost is easy to make and easy to use.

What is Composting?

Put very simply, composting is the heaping up of moist organic matter such as fresh and dry vegetative waste and waiting for the stuff to decompose into humus. Producing compost can take several weeks or months. Modern commercial composting requires several closely monitored procedures and accurately measured amounts of carbon and nitrogen-rich organic material, water and air. For organic matter to properly decompose, the bulky plant matter needs to be shredded or chopped down into smaller bits, moistened and aerated.

Worms, fungi and a variety of microorganisms help break up the organic matter. These living creatures need air, that's why a compost heap needs to be regularly turned. Composting is one of the simplest and most cost-effective ways of transforming your garden and kitchen waste into natural fertilizer. By making your own compost, you can help revitalize your garden soil or your containerized plants.

Composting is a method for treating solid waste in which organic material is broken down by microorganisms in the presence of oxygen to a point where it can be safely stored, handled and applied to the environment. The simple act of composting is an essential part of reducing household wastes. It can be done inexpensively by every household and produces a product -- finished compost or humus -- that can benefit the environment as a natural fertilizer for gardening and farming.

From the time of Pliny the Elder (AD 23-79) in the early Roman Empire, composting has been a recognized practice. Ancient farmers traditionally piled up farm residues and left the fields fallow until the next planting season. In temperate climates this composting method required little labor and working time, so it worked well with the normal agricultural practices. However, the compost heaps in the fields left fallow occupying valuable crop space for an entire year. At that time, the world's population was still relatively small, so there was little pressure to use land for intensive food production.

Ancient open-field composting required minimal inputs. Neighbors or families helped out with farm chores. Crop residues were left in piles to decompose in the fields. Exposure to the elements such as rain and snow caused some nutrients to leach out and get washed away. Rodents, insects and disease-causing organisms often abounded in the heaped-up piles. Leaving plant matter in the open fields to decay and decompose is a common practice in many parts of the world. Farmers carted dung from stables, worked this into straw and other farm stubble and left these mounds to rot. The decomposed heaps were then scattered over the fields and plowed under before the new crops were planted.

What are the different types of composting?

Aerated (turned) windrow composting

"Windrows" are long piles of organic waste laid out in the field. These long rows, 14 to 16 feet wide, are turned manually or mechanically from time to time to aerate them. Windrows need to be between 4 and 8 feet high for them to be sufficiently hot and still allow oxygen to reach the core. Aerated windrow composting accommodates huge quantities of organic wastes such as those generated by sizeable communities and businesses that process high volumes of food such as packing plants, restaurants and cafeterias.

Diverse wastes such as yard trimmings, animal byproducts, grease, liquids or slurry are incorporated in windrows that are turned frequently and carefully monitored by municipal environment agencies. Sturdy equipment and labor are needed. In cold climates, the outside portions of windrows may freeze but the core can maintain 140° F. To retain the moisture in windrows, shelters are sometimes built over the whole lengths of the windrows.

During the rainy seasons, the piles are adjusted to allow water to drain off instead of seeping into the heap. Aerated windrow composting is a large-scale operation that requires proper environmental measures to address issues such as leachate that might contaminate ground and surface-water supplies, control of odors and pest infestation, community zoning and other public health concerns. Windrow composting yields huge amounts of compost that some local governments give for free or very little cost to encourage more residents to do organic gardening.

Aerated static pile composting

Instead of rows, organic waste is mixed together in one large pile with loose layers of bulking agents such as wood chips and shredded cardboard or newspaper for aeration. Some large-scale aerated static pile composters use a network of pipes to aerate the compost heaps. The pipes deliver air into the pile and also draw air out to maintain the core temperature. Timers or programmed temperature sensors activate these air blowers.

This type of composting works well for bulk organic wastes of the same type such as sawmill sawdust or maize cob-extrusions from commercial millers. It is also suitable for huge quantities of yard trimmings and organic solid waste such as food scraps and paper products. Aerated static pile composting, unlike aerated windrow composting, is not ideal for composting grease and liquid fats from food processing industries or animal byproducts such as those from meat processing plants or abattoirs.

The strategy to minimize evaporation is similar to windrow composting where the heaps are covered or sheltered from direct exposure to the sun. Aerated static piles retain their core warmth but the passive airflow may sometimes prove challenging during cold months. Some composters resort to placing the static piles indoors and installing proper ventilation to aerate the heaps. The piles are carefully checked from time to time to insure that the outside and core temperatures are maintained. Composters using this method may apply a thick layer of mature compost over the pile to maintain high temperatures and also alleviate unpleasant odors. Aerated static pile composting can produce compost within three to six months.

Backyard or onsite composting

Homeowners, small businesses and backyard garden enthusiasts can reduce their organic disposal costs by onsite composting. Yard trimmings and a wide variety of fresh food scraps can be composted right on the property. Commercial establishments and large institutions such as hospitals, universities and prisons that generate huge quantities of food scraps may compost in situ if their campuses are big enough to allocate the space needed. When lawns are mowed regularly, the grass clippings can be left on the lawn to decompose naturally. This is known as grasscycling - the grass cuttings decay and enrich the turf. Onsite composters may rake up leaves into piles, and leave them to use later as mulch.

Very little time or equipment is required for backyard or onsite composting. Local residents may wish to educate one another by sharing composting tips and techniques. Or they can organize composting demonstrations and seminars to educate and encourage their neighbors or businesses in their community to compost on their own properties. Converting organic material to compost may take as long as two years. Manual turning can accelerate the decomposition significantly to less than 6 months or less.

Compost Tea

Beneficial microbes are extracted from vermicompost and other types of high-density microbial compost. Compost tea is made by steeping or soaking compost in water for three days to a week. Water, air, food and comfort are the four essentials for microbes to flourish. The water used for compost tea must be clean and de-chlorinated. Pure drinking (potable) water is perfect. Air is mixed into the "brewing" by a system of pipes that delivers oxygen to the microbes. Packaged nutrient mixes are added to the liquid to feed the colonies of fungi and bacteria.

The "brewed" tea is sprayed on seedlings, on the non-edible parts of vegetation or it is worked into the soil as drench to treat root tips. The microbes get down to work to suppress disease and help the soil to retain moisture and nutrients. Compost tea controls some fungal plant diseases on plant leaves so it can replace some toxic garden pesticides and fungicides.

Once the beneficial microbes are sprayed on the plant surfaces, they establish "squatters' rights" - they leave no room for pathogens (disease-causing microorganisms) to infect the plant. The microbes in compost tea produce plant growth hormones that boost healthier plant growth. These microscopic organisms mineralize some nutrients that are readily absorbed by the plants and the soil.

Leaf-mould tea or green manure tea

Some leguminous plants like beans, peanuts, soybeans and other perennials are rich in nitrogen. A nutritious "tea" is made from the leaves of such plants. Many crop leaves and wild greens such as comfrey and tithonia (wild sunflower species) may also be used to make leaf-mould tea. To make leaf-mould tea, a small pile of shredded or mashed-up leaves is wrapped in cheesecloth, burlap or any suitable material, including nylon netting. The packet is immersed in a large bucket of water. If the leaf packet threatens to float, it is weighed down with a rock or some bricks. It is left for three days or longer to steep or to brew. The "tea bag" is unwrapped and the contents are dumped into the compost heap. Leaf-mould or green manure tea is splashed directly on plants. This tea is mild so it doesn't burn young plants, even seedlings.

Vermicomposting

Vermicomposting uses worms to break down organic matter in compost bins. Ordinary earthworms in the garden could be used (if you have the patience to dig them up and transfer them into the bin). A variety of worm species including earthworms, white worms and red wigglers are used to produce vermicast. The worm poop, called castings, are high-value compost. This high-quality end-product is also known as worm manure, worm castings and worm humus. (Paper on Invasive Worms)

Vermiculture experts prefer red wigglers because they are voracious eaters and they breed fast. Compared to conventional composting, vermicomposting produces compost quicker as worms convert organic matter to usable end-product faster. When earthworms digest their food, they mix up minerals and nutrients into simple forms that are easy for plants to absorb. Beneficial microbes in the worms' digestive tract help to efficiently break down food particles that eventually enrich the soil. Vermicast is less saline so it can be applied directly to plants without risking "burning" sensitive plant parts. (Lazcano, Gomez-Brandon and Dominguez 2008)

You can buy commercially available worm bins or you can construct your own from scrap lumber or discarded tubs. People who don't have yards can do vermicomposting successfully in their apartments or small offices. Worms will consume almost everything in a typical compost pile - plants, moistened paper, food scraps, etc. Vermicomposting is a great way for schools to demonstrate to children how to manage organic solid waste, conserve resources and to recycle.

Aside from insuring that they are adequately fed, keep your worms healthy and alive by checking that they are not subjected to extreme temperatures. The ideal temperature for vermicomposting is between 55° F to 77° F (12.80C to 250C). If you live in hot, arid areas, keep the worm bids in the shade. Indoor vermicomposting eliminates many of the challenges of too hot or too cold climates. Use shredded newspaper or cardboard for worm bedding. Add the organic matter which serves as worm food.

How much can worms eat in a day? A pound of mature worms can consume up to half a pound of organic matter per day. So a worm can eat the equivalent of half its weight in a single day. Separate the worms when you "harvest" the castings. Worms can produce enough harvestable castings after three to four months. You can use the castings as potting soil or you can be more sparing, apply the castings like compost. A side product of vermicomposting is "worm" tea, produced much like leafmould tea. Wrap castings in burlap or cheesecloth, immerse in water for some time, then use the high-quality liquid as fertilizer for your house pants.

In-vessel composting

This large-scale operation requires expensive concrete-lined trenches, silos, sturdy drums and similar equipment to contain the organic matter to be composted. Aeration, moisture and temperature are vigilantly monitored, often electronically. Unlike the weather constraints of windrow and static pile composting, in-vessel composting can be done in all and even extreme climatic conditions with proper insulation.

A mechanism in the composting vessel turns or agitates the organic matter to aerate it properly. Large volumes of any organic waste including biosolids, animal manure, food scraps and meat or other animal byproducts can be accommodated in in-vessel composters. The vessels vary in size, some as large as a school bus and others small enough to fit into a restaurant or school kitchen.

Minimal leachate, very little odor, less land and manual labor are the pluses of in-vessel composting that may offset the initial high cost of the vessels and the required technical expertise. Organic matter decomposes in a few weeks but once out of the composting vessel, the pile needs to cool first before it can be used. It might take some weeks for the microbial activity in the compost to stabilize.

In addition to the traditional compost pile, various composting approaches have been developed in many parts of the world. These alternative composting methods and techniques are adapted to suit locations, available organic matter or compost ingredients and the specific applications for the different end-products.

Grub composting

This is a very fast technique for making compost. Black soldier flies are kept in "cages" where they lay their eggs. The eggs hatch into larvae or grubs. Enthusiasts and breeders say grub composting can be done in the garage, the bedroom and even the kitchen because the bins are sanitary and the whole operation is basically odorless and tidy. Grubs quickly convert kitchen waste and animal manure into usable compost. Grubs are at least 50 times more efficient than earthworms and other wigglers at composting waste.

It could be fascinating to watch masses of these creepy crawlies devour huge quantities of organic waste such as fruit peel and food scraps, meat and even animal manure. Chopping and shredding would not be necessary. The voracious grubs are incredible eating machines - they consume almost everything, including rotting vegetation dumped into the bins. The sawdust-like and odorless grub poop is called fry, a useful compost residue. Earthworms love grub poop.

Black soldier flies are large and slow-moving. They resemble wasps. Unlike common houseflies, soldier flies do not carry germs and they do not bite. They love sunlight so they don't want to stay indoors. Commercial BSF breeders provide specially designed traps to keep the investment from flying away and to have them lay the eggs where they are supposed to. Soldier flies live only a few days. After mating, they lay their eggs and die within hours. The eggs hatch into larvae, also known as soldier grubs. In a grub bin, there is a separate collection container where the mature grubs crawl into. This is hands off harvesting!

At 42% protein and 34% fat, soldier grubs are nutritious feed for poultry, pigs, turtles, pond fish and other non-vegetarian farm animals. Given to animals live or dried, grubs can significantly reduce the expense for commercial grade feed. Sport fishermen and neophyte anglers love to use grubs as live bait.
Among other benefits that Jerry Gach, The Worm Dude, enumerates, soldier grubs are "self-separating, auto-harvesting, robust, prolific, hardy, indigenous, harmless, easy-to-store, simple to transport, dry to the touch in pupal stage, a convenient bait, and extremely nutritious". Also, grubs that are actively feeding "secrete a natural fly repellant called a synomone (an interspecies, chemical communication that alerts and warns other kinds of flies to stay away". (thewormdude.com)

Cockroach composting

Yes, cockroaches are amazingly efficient composters. Cockroaches can eat anything and everything, they reproduce like crazy, need only super-low maintenance and they don't smell. Cockroaches are difficult to kill except by using disastrous chemicals. You may find it disgusting to think of raising cockroaches to do composting, but, it's true, these hardy insects can convert kitchen waste and even manure into compost much faster than the traditional compost heap.

Species such as the Turkestan cockroach or Blaptica dubia, Blatta lateralis and others are used. While cockroaches produce fewer droppings than other invertebrates used for composting, the castings are more nutrient-dense. At different stages, cockroaches molt and the chitin from the molts boosts the quality of the compost. Excess insects can be fed to farm animals and pets like bearded dragons, geckos and some birds.

Cockroach composting is unconventional, weird and freaky. One has to overcome the initial disgust to cockroaches. But, the efficiency of these disgusting insects makes up for the prejudice targeted at them. A discarded aquarium tank or any large-enough container can be used as cockroach bins. All kinds of food can be tossed into the cockroach breeding pen - nasty moldy food, dog food, people food - all leftovers. Prolific breeders, a cockroach colony can grow at astonishing speed. Each capsule-looking egg case contains 20 to 30 eggs.

Other creatures like darkling beetles, sparrows, geckos and some crickets get attracted to cockroach bins. Beetles eat up what the roaches don't, so nature works perfectly to create richer compost of the bedding substrate. The bedding turns moist and thick from cockroach and beetle frass and other decomposed material such as brittle bones and crumbling shells. Frass is a general term for insect poop and may also include the chitin-rich shed exoskeletons.
Glued-together egg cartons in the bins make cozy homes for cockroaches - they love the dark compartments. The cleaned out bedding in cockroach bins are super-rich in nutrients. Before it is used in the garden, the bedding is normally put in sealed containers or subjected to heat to kill off the beetle larvae and the cockroach egg cases. This compost is so rich that it is mixed with traditional compost. (gilcarandang.com)

Hügelkultur

In German, hügelkultur roughly translates as "mound culture". Rotting wood is the base of hugelkultur. This gardening and farming technique mimicking natural woodland "recycling" of nutrients has been used in eastern Europe for hundreds of years. Woody debris and all types of detritus act like sponges while decomposing - soaking up and retaining rainwater. Crops planted on the mounds use the moisture slowly released by the buried woody "sponges". (richsoil.com and Hemenway 2009)

Like traditional compost heaps, hugelkultur beds release heat for several years, thus fruit trees in inhospitable altitudes and temperatures survive by this method of horticulture. Woody debris, otherwise unsuitable for other types of composting, improves on-site drainage and improves the fertility of compacted soils. Simply defined, hugelkultur garden beds are large woody compost piles with layers of carbon and nitrogen-rich debris.

A simple hugelkultur bed could be 6 feet long and 3 feet wide but there is no fixed rule on sizing. Fallen logs, the largest of the biomass debris, are loosely laid out for the first layer. Next, branches are added upon which small twigs and sticks are evenly layered. Manure, kitchen scraps, leaf litter and any other organic matter available are worked into the spaces between the logs, twigs and branches.

Layers are watered sufficiently if the mounds are set up during the dry season. The mound could be 3 feet high but it is up to the gardener's discretion and patience, really. A two-inch layer of dirt tops the mound. Mulching material like straw and shredded leaves covers the soil layer. It is best to allow hugelkultur garden beds to "cure" a bit before they are planted. In temperate climates, the beds can be laid out in the fall in time for spring planting. However, with sufficient moisture, seeds and seedlings can be planted shortly after the mounds are built - when the organic matter has at least decomposed a little.

"Humanure"

Humanure should not be mistaken for night soil, the raw human excreta collected at night from cesspools and privies and applied on field crops as fertilizer. An alternative definition of "night soil" is the primitive, albeit sanitary, "dig and cover" method. A person goes into the maize or any tall crop field at night, digs a shallow hole, deposits his excrement, and covers it up. If not dug up by scavengers, the raw human waste serves its purpose of fertilizing the standing crops. Humanure is basically a combination of human feces and urine with carbon material such as paper and sawdust. Joseph Jenkins (2005) first used "humanure" in his 1994 book where he advocated this type of eco-friendly soil enrichment.

For those who still feel barfy at the thought of their fresh salad greens, reds and yellows grown on humanure - relax! Humanure must pass certain public health standards before it is commercially used on crops. Most crops fertilized with humanure are those not eaten raw. These could be non-food crops like cotton, sisal or crops adapted to arid conditions where the sun kills off most of the remaining bacteria.

Human excrement in a compost toilet is collected and mixed into a hot compost heap of sawdust, straw and other carbon matter. Properly managed, a compost toilet will not stink. The heat and the possible addition of chemicals kill off pathogens in the compost mixture. Humanure composting is done "on location" or in situ. News reporters sometimes incorrectly use the "humanure" synonymously with "biosolids" or "sewer sludge" which does not help dispel public hostility to the term. (Symons 2011)

Despite its unattractive name, humanure offers eco-friendly advantages. Human waste is rich in nitrogen, calcium, phosphorus, carbon and potassium - rivaling a number of commercially available fertilizers and composts. Unlike flush toilets that demand large amounts of water, compost toilets are "dry" operations. The decomposition of fecal matter is controlled so the waste does not pollute or contaminate ground water. When composted in accordance with health regulations on pathogen destruction and adequate curing, humanure is safe for crops.

Municipal solid waste (MSW) co-composting

Urban communities resort to large-scale composting systems to handle the voluminous wastes generated daily. Solid waste is combined with de-watered biosolids in co-composting technique. This approach to municipal solid waste management faces the difficulties of controlling inert and plastics contamination. The Edmonton Composting Facility in Edmonton, Alberta, Canada is the largest MSW co-composter in the world. It turns close to 250,000 tonnes of residential solid waste and biosolids into 80,000 tonnes of compost per year.

The operating structure, the size of 14 NHL rinks, is the largest stainless steel building in North America. (Edmonton composting facility)
Environmental concerns over hazardous landfill gases prompt countries to adopt more advanced industrial composting systems. In several places, biodegradable waste is mechanically sorted and treated before it enters landfills to reduce anaerobic decomposition that contribute to harmful greenhouse gases.

"Super-charged" rapid organic waste composting

Rapid composting techniques have been developed to balance out the challenges faced by traditional, slow composting. A number of modern scientists are skeptical about techniques that force or manipulate nature to make compost so rapidly. However, other scientists, driven by necessity and demand, have experimented and devised mechanisms to do "super-charged" composting of large volumes of organic waste. Densely-populated countries, like India, came up with the Excel Organic Waste Convertor (OWC). This method turns ready-to-use compost within 10 incredible days.

The Excel organic waste converter works like this: organic waste is sorted or segregated. It is fed into the OWC - which grinds it into fine particles. Bioculum and absorbent are added into the grinded organic matter. The treated mass is placed into the curing system. Voila! In just 10 days the compost is ready for the kitchen garden.

Excel markets complete OWC components and the needed accelerators. Its website (excelind.co.in) describes bioculum as "a mixture of micro organism cultures that accelerate the aerobic composting of bio degradable organic waste. It also treats the waste and makes it free from pathogens, foul smells and weed seeds.

Bioculum is a key input in the OWC process and consists of cultures of naturally occurring bacteria, fungi and actinomycitis along with enzymes. These facilitate the rapid conversion of organic waste into a bio-stabilized compost. It is free from any toxic or hazardous components. It preserves the vital nutrients and organic matter in the waste".

WHAT ARE THE ETHICAL AND ENVIRONMENTAL CONCERNS OVER ORGANIC WASTE?

Responsible ecological stewardship - how can we foster it? It starts with us. Individual action on a daily basis - from the time we get up, to the time we retire for the day. The children growing up among us learn from our example. They will continue caring for Mother Earth well into the next few decades. Are we addressing the serious environmental concerns that impact generations to come?

Cities around the world take decisive environmental measures to cope with the stench and hazards of overflowing landfills. "Green bin" programs encourage residents to put out organic waste in separate containers for curbside collection. San Francisco requires all residents through its "Mandatory Recycling and Composting Ordinance," to sort their trash into "recyclables, compostables and landfill trash". Many cities have followed San Francisco's lead. Close to 40% of San Francisco's trash that went to landfills was compostable kitchen and plant waste - this was before the ordinance was enacted. A million tons of organic waste has been converted to compost since the city implemented its mandatory recycling and composting ordinance. (homeguides.sfgate.com)

When we convert organic waste into compost, we are being good stewards of the earth. Composting is one single act we can do that will leave a positive footprint on the ecosystem.

Composting renders economic and social benefits

Large food-catering businesses such as restaurants and hospital/university canteens can more effectively plan their food purchases to minimize waste. This applies to households too. We buy more food than we actually need and the fridge and pantry groan from the overload. We efficiently reduce labor and garbage disposal cost when we compost more quantities of trash. Food banks and charities that run food rescue operations welcome donations of wholesome excess foods from well-wishers. Instead of feeding the landfills and smelly garbage dumps, we can feed those in need. In some countries, citizens can claim tax benefits when they donate healthy and safe foods to food banks or charitable agencies.(EPA)

Composting helps landfills from filling up prematurely

Large quantities of vegetable matter and other organics utilized in home and large-scale commercial composting are kept out of landfills. Composting slows down the loading up of landfills and helps to reduce pollution. The air-less or anaerobic environment inside the landfills generates methane gas which is more potent than carbon dioxide. Methane harms the Earth's atmosphere. Hardly any methane is generated when organic waste is composted above the ground as oxygen helps the waste to decompose naturally.

Every person can do his little bit to reduce waste sent to landfills. Rubbish bins contain a lot of good stuff that can be composted to help build healthier soils. Instead of sending organic waste into landfills, it can be composted conventionally or by anaerobic means. Composting converts organic waste into renewable energy such as biogas through anaerobic digestion. The sludge and slurry, by-products of large-scale anaerobic biogas production, make good composting material. Bokashi is an example of small-scale but also scalable anaerobic composting gaining popularity in many parts of the world.

Composting feeds the soil

Humans depend on the soil for most of the crops they use for food, building materials, fiber and other needs. The soil, so generous and forgiving even as it is exploited to the max, needs to be replenished. Susan Peterson writes: "Jared Eliot, in his classic 1748 book "Essays Upon Field Husbandry," introduced an often-cited metaphor. The soil, he said, is like a bank. A person who grows food in the soil without returning plant wastes and manure to it is like a person who repeatedly withdraws cash from a bank account without ever making a deposit. Composting food waste, then returning that compost to fields and gardens, allows us to return nutrients to the soil bank that feeds us."

Composting improves the soil

Applying compost to compacted soils helps moisture to seep in slowly instead of running off as it does on a bare, compacted surface. This loosens the hard soils and allows plants to establish roots that in turn release nutrients even as they absorb these from the soil. Compost improves the capacity of sandy soils and other porous soils to retain water, thus making crop-irrigation more cost-effective.

Composting minimizes chemicals

Compost acts as a natural pesticide for soil. Beneficial microorganisms in compost such as bacteria, actinobacteria, protozoa and rotifers keep one another's populations from dominating. Some harmful pests find the prolific presence of compost microbes too hostile for them to propagate. In addition to the basic nutrients supplied by chemical fertilizers - potassium, nitrogen and phosphorus, compost contains some nutrients and trace minerals that are not available in many laboratory-formulated chemical fertilizers.

Rain and irrigation often wash off excess chemical fertilizer nitrogen into the ocean, lakes and ponds. This causes algae to bloom too abundantly, using up lots of oxygen that fish and other aquatic animals need. Some chemicals, useful to plants but harmful to animals and humans contaminate sources of drinking water like springs and water wells.

Did you know that you can actually prevent, just in one year of home composting, the equivalent amount of global warming gases to all the carbon dioxide that your kettle produces, in the same amount of time or that of your washing machine in three months? Because of the lack of oxygen, organic waste in most landfills does not decompose, it rots. Rotting waste generates methane gas which is over 20 times more potent than carbon dioxide's capacity to warm the global atmosphere. (EPA)

Composting helps control erosion and check sediments

Slopes with unstable soils are prone to erosion. Using compost in such areas can help reduce the formation of gulleys and rills and prevent the further compacting of the bare soils exposed to the elements. Compost increases the amount of water that can seep into the soil instead of running off causing sheet erosion. Compost blankets and compost filter berms are the two common methods of using compost to control erosion.

Compost blankets

Compost blankets or compost mats are uniformly applied compost over wide areas of terrain prone to erosion or badly eroded surfaces that need repair. High-quality compost is spread either manually or by machinery. The 1 to 3 inches of compost is compacted into the surface by mechanical rollers or bulldozers. More compost is applied to steeper slopes with unstable soils. After the compost has been tracked or compacted, it is seeded or planted to ornamentals. As the vegetation grows, the roots help to stabilize or anchor the compost mat into the underlying soil.

Compost filter berms

Compost filter berms are dikes constructed across areas of sheet runoff to retain sediments. Compost or compost products are used for filter berms that are trapezoidal in cross-section. These three dimensional filters trap the sediment and pollutants such as oil and grease, metals and suspended solids, but allow the cleaned water to flow through. Yard trimmings, food residues, segregated solid wastes, bio-solids, manure and a variety of animal feedstock are some of the materials used to construct filter berms.

Stable organic filter berms utilize wood-based mulch, chipped site vegetation, composted mulch, and composts containing denser and variedly-sized particles.
Compost filter berms are constructed at intervals along a slope to slow down storm water. Organic filter berms help to retain large volumes of sediment in its pores or spaces while slowing down the flow of water. Berms degrade chemical pollutants before these reach bodies of water. The water quality downstream of berms is improved because heavy metals and other potentially hazardous substances are retained as water flows through the compost.

Other pollutants that are filtered through berms include nitrogen, phosphorus, herbicides, pesticides, fuel, grease and oils. Organic filter berms can be left "on-site" and are suitable places for intentional planting and wild vegetation growth. Berms can be planted or unplanted. Planted or vegetated berms are usually left in place to serve longer. Unplanted or un-vegetated berms can be broken down and the compost is used to enrich the surrounding soils.

WHAT IS HOME COMPOST GARDENING?

You may or may not have "green thumbs" but if you have even a teeny bit of front or backyard, you can try your hand at gardening. Just for the fun and the relaxation of it. Yes, fertilizers are readily available in any garden center but you can make your own soil food or enhancers at home. In all simplicity - that's home compost gardening. You make your own compost because your conscience tells you to act decisively so you care for the environment. You help eliminate food wastes biologically as you create nutrient-rich food for plants. You can adapt the appropriate features of the many types of composting already described.

Home compost gardening is not as intimidating as some timid beginners might think. A simple heap in a corner of your backyard plus some "tender loving care" is all it takes to make the natural supplement your garden plants need. When you make your own compost, you are actually helping nature replenish its depleted nutrient reserves.

You divert as much as a half or more of household waste away from the refuse bin that would eventually go to the municipal landfill or commercial composting facilities. Save your money that you would otherwise spend on chemical fertilizers or store-bought compost. Help nurse the earth back to health naturally by providing the environment for microorganisms to proliferate. These miniscule "soldiers" ward off plant disease so the need for pesticides and herbicides will reduce.

A Variety of Common Home-Composting Techniques
As a beginner, you may wish to try small-scale traditional or casual composting first. But you can jump right in and do it "gourmet style" that demands more effort and equipment from you but with quicker results.

Casual composting

An outdoor compost pile requires minimal tending. This is "lazy man's" composting: you will harvest compost after several months (or years!). The often neglected or forgotten compost can take up to two years to mature. Casual composting is a no-brainer: simply mark off a dry and shady spot in your backyard near a water source (to reduce your watering trips). Put in the mixture of greens and browns in an open heap, water now and then, turn occasionally with a shovel or pitch fork and wait. Just like that.
Because these small piles don't get too hot, you might find some critters like garden bugs and earthworms at the bottom of your heap. Keep them there, or you can dig up more of the wigglers from other parts of your backyard and push them in. They will do the aerating for you. Most casual composting is done traditionally in the open.

"No turn" composting

Turning the compost heap from time to time can sap the energies of a neophyte composter. You can aerate the compost without turning. The secret? Simply start smart: when you build up your pile, thoroughly mix in enough coarse material such as straw and dry leaves (the ones that crackle to your touch) to about equal amounts of the "greens". The bulky "browns" will allow air to circulate evenly within the heap so you don't have to turn it. Drive in several branchy stakes into your compost heap to keep your mix from flattening or matting too quickly especially in heavy rain. Eartheasy experts suggest: "With 'no-turn' composting, add new materials to the top of the pile, and harvest fresh compost from the bottom of the bin." (eartheasy.com)

How big should your compost pile be? Those who have done home composting successfully say that a heap should be at least one cubic yard (less than one cubic meter): three feet tall, three feet deep and three feet wide. This size is large enough to provide food for the microorganisms and keep them warm enough so they can happily continue propagating and working. A one cubic meter compost heap is also small enough for air to circulate within the heap - provided the ingredients are thoroughly mixed. Just check that your materials are not too chunky so the microbes will have an easier time breaking them down.

Gourmet composting

Gourmet composting, despite the glamorous name, basically uses the same principles with the added flair of using beautiful composting bins so convincingly marketed by gardening businesses. A number of gourmet composting methods utilize lab-prepared "accelerators" to speed up the decomposition of organic waste. Bokashi and the OWC home-compost units are examples of these accelerated processes. Most gourmet composting is done indoors. Gourmet composting and indoor composting can be one and the same, although there are also variations that combine the two techniques.

Manufactured composting bins come complete with stacking mechanisms, hoops, turning units, cones and other nice gadgets to entice you into turning out respectable compost. Consider buying a rotating compost tumbler if you don't want to turn your compost yourself. Gardening supplies stores have an endless variety of beautiful - even aesthetic models of gourmet compost bins. Take your pick: you can even match the motif or design of your backyard or patio - you are spoiled for choice!

Or you can opt to make your own bin. The structure does not need to be fancy, just fun and functional. You are dealing with decomposing (not rotting) organic material so the microbes don't really care if your bin is an aesthetic investment or a crudely crafted but practical creation. A typical homemade bin can be constructed out of scrap lumber, riff-raff wood from a construction site or failed woodcraft hobby, chicken wire and other suitable material you find in the house. Old garbage cans, a discarded bathtub or any large-enough container would do. Punch holes on the sides and bottom for drainage. A wooden composting bin might attract termites, so you can stand the legs in tin cans filled with used engine oil or similar sticky liquid.

To insure your compost aerates properly, you can "nest" a smaller bin inside a larger container. You can convert a discarded bathtub into a "mother bin": place several bricks at the bottom, layer wood chips and soil in between the bricks and place smaller containers on top. Check that these have drainage holes. Your creative genius can turn unsightly compost tubs into pleasantly eye-catching corners of your backyard.

Compost bins can be attractive decorative features of your garden, patio or deck. If space is limited and you don't want to display your homemade bins, you can creatively screen them from view. Put your artistic touch on a bamboo, wattle or willow fencing or trellis and allow climbing plants to naturally embellish it. Recycle.now.com offers helpful tips on the sites for your compost bins.

On wire mesh. Scrape out or dig a one or two-inch deep hole that matches the diameter of your bin. Place a wire mesh slightly larger than the base of your bin. One or two bricks or stones in the hole could nicely keep your mesh from sagging under the weight of the compost bin. The wire mesh can help keep unwanted vermin out from your compost.

On paving. If it does not disturb or alter the looks of your courtyard too much, remove some of the paving. The leachate or liquid that seep out of the bottom of the compost bin may stain whatever is beneath it. Alternatively, keep the paving intact but construct a small raised bed. Line several bricks or similar-shaped rocks in a circle or square. Fill it with a mixture of soil, gravel or other coarse and porous material. This improvised bed will contain the leachate from your bin. It is also a nice, cozy home for earthworms and other soil-dwelling critters. This method also works well if you must put your bins on concrete.

On decking. You don't have a paved courtyard but you have a deck. Build a non-staining raised bed on top of your deck. Compliment your deck with matching deckboards for your raised bed. To be on the safe side, use decking seal on the deckboards and cover with plastic to prevent staining from leachate. Fill the raised bed with soil to absorb any liquid seeping out of the compost bin. Leachate is great liquid feed for the plants you put into the raised "catching" bed.

On gravel. Your compost bins will sit nicely on gravel. The gravel could be in your garden, a side path or a corner of a gravel driveway. Cut slits or punch holes in the membrane underneath the gravel if this has been laid out previously. This allows microbes to access your compost bins. Lay out a plastic sheet to keep compost mess from "dirtifying" your gravel when you empty the contents of your bin.

Bokashi composting

Bokashi is a ramped-up, high-speed and intensive composting method first developed in Japan. Compost is ready in a matter of days, unlike in traditional composting that takes months to produce mature compost. The term "bokashi" is Japanese for "fermented organic matter". Efficient microbes (EM) are used in this anaerobic type of composting. Centuries ago, Japanese farmers covered food waste with layers of microbe-rich garden soil to mitigate foul smells. The microorganisms in the soil caused the food waste to ferment for several weeks. The farmers buried the fermented food waste which turned into soil weeks later. (Lindsay 2012)

Fermentation is bokashi's muscle; it is what ordinary compost lacks. Microbes that thrive without oxygen decompose organic matter in bokashi composting. Bokashi is a simple and tidy composting technique. Although food waste ferments, bokashi is normally odorless, when managed properly. Bokashi suits people who live in apartments or condos and those who wish speedier breakdown of organic waste. Small-scale bokashi composting can be done in an ordinary home or scaled-up for large volumes of kitchen waste in schools, restaurants, and other large institutions that generate lots of food scraps. Buckets can be fitted with wheels for easy transport.

To start bokashi, you would need at least two big containers with tight-fitting lids, kitchen scraps, houseplants debris and bokashi mix. This powdery mix contains molasses, wheat bran and EMs – the efficient microorganisms that basically drive this anaerobic composting process. One handful of bokashi mix to every 2 inches of food waste. There is no hard and fast rule on how much bokashi mix you can add - better too much than too little. Keep the bin closed tightly after every addition of composting materials.

Repeat the layering until the bucket is full. Let contents ferment for up to two weeks. A commercial bokashi bin has a drainage spout at the bottom. Bokashi juice is a terrific fertilizer - just remember to dilute it before applying to your plants. It is pretty strong so even when diluted, don't apply it directly to foliage. One teaspoon to about three liters of water for garden and house plants and 2 teaspoons to about three liters for trees and shrubs. Pour bokashi juice down drains to check slime build-up and foul smells. Bokashi juice loses potency after a few days so use it within that period.

A sweet-sour pickle-like "aroma" and a whitish growth on the surface of the composting waste indicate that your stuff is fermenting nicely. After about two weeks, take the bokashi compost out of the bucket and bury it in the garden. Take care not to get the fresh bokashi stuff to come in direct contact with plants, even the roots as they could "burn". Wait for about 2 weeks more before you put in your favorite veggies or flowers into soil enriched with bokashi compost.

WHAT CAN YOU COMPOST?

What you can compost: four essential ingredients

Air + Water + Carbon + Nitrogen: these are the essential ingredients in a compost heap. When you compost, you are simply recreating what nature does all the time. You step up the decomposition process by manipulating conditions to speed up the breaking down of organic matter. Blending roughly equal parts of dry and wet organic material is the easiest compost recipe. When in doubt or unsure about the dry and wet matter ratio, it is better to have more of the dry than of the wet. Maintaining a working balance between the carbon-rich and nitrogen-rich materials is the secret to a healthy compost pile.

The Greens: Nitrogen-rich organic materials

Nitrogen or protein-rich matter provides the raw ingredients to produce enzymes. The tiny organisms that break down organic matter need the proteins to build up their microscopic bodies. Microbes need nitrogen to grow and reproduce. In the composting process, microorganisms oxidize the bulky carbon in the compost mix. Organic matter that are rich in nitrogen and protein are generally wet or moist green plant matter, this is why they are referred to as greens. In reality, however, nitrogen-rich materials include animal by-products such as manure. So although these ingredients are called greens, they can be red, yellow, green, brown - and all the colors in between.

Manure from cows or horses, chickens and turkeys is rich in nitrogen and heats up compost piles very well. Grass and landscape trimmings, vegetable and fruit peels and pulp and other kitchen scraps are nitrogen-laden. More brown to green is the rule of thumb: two-thirds brown matter and one-third green stuff. Too much of greens can turn the compost heap into a dense and smelly mass that takes too long to decompose.

The Browns: Carbon-rich organic materials

Bulky brown organic materials allow oxygen to penetrate the compost heap. The microbes that reside in the pile oxidize the carbon-rich ingredients. The browns include shredded brown paper bags and cardboard, egg shells, peat moss, straw, wood ash, corn stalks and dead leaves. All other dry organic matter such as sawdust, twigs and branches, bark, dry leaves and untreated wood chips are carbon sources that make compost fluffy and light.
Again, as with the greens, organic carbon-rich matter are usually brown but could have widely varying shades of yellows and whites. Microbes utilize carbon-rich material for energy.

Carbon is a very essential component in compost heaps but too much of it can also slow down decomposition or lock it to a standstill altogether. Australian "Cleanup" puts this reality in focus: "If you have a pile with mostly prunings from your hedge and other woody stuff, the pile can take years to break down. It can sit there and linger in your back yard and you may begin to make plans to will your compost to your grandchildren." (cleanup.au)

Water

A most common mistake of beginner composters is the extreme of too much and too little water. They either leave the heap to get too dry or they drench the mix into a soggy heap. Compost microbes need just the right amount of moisture. Too much water will make the heap too cold and reduce the flow of air. This results in smelly compost. Too little water hampers the breaking down of the organic waste (imagine the microbes too thirsty and listless to perform their tasks).

The compost mix will not heat up if it is too dry. Remember that within the compost heap, an active community of little critters are busy breaking down, digesting and ingesting the organic matter so they need to be hydrated. The decomposing organic matter in the compost heap "should be moist as a wrung-out sponge". Expert composters prefer 40 to 60 percent moisture content: very few drops of water (or none at all) come out when a handful of compost is squeezed. In dry weather, more watering may be done to keep the mix moist enough. Piles in the open field need to be covered during the rainy season. Alternatively, the heaps can be constructed in a way that excess water can drain off instead of it seeping into the pile and making it soggy.

Air

It is important for compost to be porous - to allow air inside the heap. Pores or spaces inside the pile allow in oxygen for the bacteria and fungus that are breaking down the compost mix. When the compost heap is too dense or too wet, the oxygen supply is cut off and the beneficial microbes will die. This causes the pile to stink and greenhouse gases are generated. Turn and fluff the heap with a pitchfork at least once a week or once in a fortnight (two weeks). Re-fluffing the material improves the airflow and moves new compost material into the center of the pile. It is natural for once fluffy piles to compress during the composting process. Break up a flat, matted compost pile and mix in new greens and browns to activate decomposition.

Other Composting Ingredients

Manure and bedding

On many livestock farms, straw and sawdust are used for bedding. In some places where straw and sawdust are in short supply, some non-traditional bedding materials are used. These include crunched up newspaper, chopped or torn-up cardboard, shredded office paper and residues or dry wastes from paper mills. Animal manures differ in composition and composting quality. Swine manure, generally very wet, requires huge quantities of straw. Normally, bedding is not provided for swine as their pens are washed or flushed often. The manure of cattle, sheep, goats and horses is good for commercial compost mixes. Poultry manure is super-rich, especially with birds raised in battery cages or the "force-fed" broilers. Chicken dung requires curing, even when mixed with carbonaceous organic matter, before being applied to vegetation. (Dougherty 1999)

Urine

Human urine contains more potassium, nitrogen and potassium than feces. Plants utilize these nutrients for growth. A healthy person's urine is effective directly applicable fertilizer. When added to compost, urine increases the temperatures which helps destroy unwanted seeds and pathogens. Urine from a healthy person does not contain parasitic worm eggs so it is more sanitary than fresh feces. When diluted, urine usually does not stink and can be used directly on non-edible plants such as shrubbery and ornamentals. The urea in urine is good for plants but care should be taken not to over-fertilize plants with urine. (Winker 2009)

Microorganisms

With all the essential composting ingredients in place, the major composting job can be turned over to microorganisms.

Over time, both aerobic and anaerobic microbes break down all composted material. Hosts of these active critters, with the right amounts of nitrogen, carbon, oxygen and water flourish in the compost heap. Among the most common microorganisms that work actively in compost are bacteria, molds and yeast, actinobacteria, protozoa and rotifers.

Bacteria are the most prolific. Molds and yeast are fungi that break down matter too tough for bacteria such as the lignin in wood. Other harder stuff like bark, wood shavings and paper products are broken down by actinobacteria. Populations of bacteria and fungi are efficiently controlled by simple-celled protozoa, keeping a balance in the micro-environment. Rotifers keep protozoans from dominating. Earthworms dig tunnels through the compost that help aerate the decomposing mass and prevent excess liquid build-up. Wigglers consume large quantities of the organic matter and produce high-quality end-product: vermicast or worm manure.

Landfills do not have healthy populations of beneficial microorganisms. This explains why the mountains of garbage take too long to decompose. The compacted trash and waste in landfills lack the oxygen and other conditions for these helpful biological composting agents to work effectively.

Soil

Most soils host an abundance of microorganisms. Adding garden soil to the compost mix introduces or adds to the community of biological composters. A layer of soil on top of a compost heap masks odors, keep flies and other vermin at bay and helps to regulate the temperature of the decomposing mass.

What can you compost? Here's a handy list!
Rule of thumb for beginners: 50% greens **and** 50%

browns in your compost.	
The Greens (nitrogen-rich material) These materials rot quickly and they provide important nitrogen and moisture.	**The Browns (carbon-rich material)** These materials are slower to rot. They allow air pockets to form in your compost.
animal manure with straw annual weeds remains before they have set seed annual crops residues bindweed bracken brussels sprout stalk carrot tops citrus peel coffee grounds and filters comfrey leaves cut flowers, dead flowers deadly nightshade fruit peelings, pulp, seeds fruits and vegetables (discarded) fruit and vegetable scraps, peelings, grass mowing, cuttings, clippings hay hedge clippings house plants ivy leaves nettles old bedding plants old potting mix perennial weeds	autumn or fallen leaves cardboard (torn up) christmas tree corn starch liners cotton towels cotton wool, cotton rags dryer lint egg boxes eggshells evergreen prunings human and animal hair, fur natural corks nuts, nut shells paper bags privet sawdust (from untreated timber) scrunched up paper shredded newspaper straw sweetcorn cobs thorny prunings tomato plants

plant debris, weeds poisonous plants rhubarb leaves seaweed soft prunings, soft stems tea leaves and tea bags urine	used kitchen paper used vegetable cooking oil vacuum cleaner dust, lint, contents wood ash, fireplace ashes wood chips wool, wool rags, wool scraps

What you cannot compost: THE REDS - Keep these stuff out!

black walnut tree leaves or twigs coal or charcoal ash dairy products (e.g., butter, milk, sour cream, yogurt) diseased or insect-ridden plants: fats, grease, lard, or oils meat and fish bones, scraps pet wastes such as dog or cat feces trimmings from hedges/gardens treated with chemical pesticides rhubarb leaves (may be toxic to some organisms in the soil) invasive plants or weeds with persistent root systems or seeds fruit peels and rind that may still have pesticide residue perennial	animal manures (especially the droppings of cats and dogs) bones bread cans cat litter cigarette ends cling film cooked food (including cake, cookies) crisp packets dairy products diseased plants disposable nappies dog food drink cartons fat magazines large branches

weeds such as bindweed plastic: bags, bottles sawdust from treated timber soiled tissues weeds that have seeds or underground stems	meat and fish scraps metals, glass olive oil

Recognize when some things are out of kilter with your compost.
Do a little tweaking!

Something is wrong!	How you can fix it.
Your compost smells. The heap is not aerated enough or there is too much "greens" that give your mix a bit too much moisture.	Turn the pile and fork in more dry material such as mulch, dry leaves, shredded paper or straw. If your compost is smelling "sour", you can add woodfire ash, garden lime and calcium to neutralize the acidity and the odors. Check

	that you left out bones or meat scraps as these are sure to stink!
Pests and vermin such as cockroaches, slugs, mice or rats have invaded your compost heap. Bones, starchy and fatty foods, animal feces are magnets for rodents, vermin and even the house pets. Flies, beetles, bees, ants, crickets, wasps and a horde of creepy crawlies are attracted to your compost.	Bury the tempting fresh food scraps deep inside the heap. Add a layer of garden soil or shredded dry leaves on top of the compost to discourage flies. Slugs love the moist and warmth of your mix. Use garden tongs to remove them and their eggs that look like pearl clusters. You can keep the rats and mice from the compost heap by fine wire. Use your ingenuity at designing traps from whatever available materials you have at hand. Turn the pile at least once a week to disturb the unwelcome residents. Keep fruit and vegetable matter covered by an inch or two of clippings.
Your compost takes too long to mature. It is not hot enough or the compost pile is too dry and lacks air or water or both. The carbons and nitrogen-rich materials may not be properly balanced. Maybe your pile is too small to retain enough	Your compost heap should be at least 3 feet high, 3 feet wide and 3 feet long to generate enough heat. See that there is roughly a half-half mix of the greens and browns. Sprinkle or finely spray water

heat.	evenly through the heap - but do not drench! Turn the heap and mix the contents well. Add handfuls of soil. Cover the heap and let it sit for a week. During the long winter months, you can insulate your compost heap to make sure it doesn't get too cold. A heavy porous mantle like natural fiber matting or burlap would work just fine. You can also speed up the composting process by adding an "accelerator". Finely-shredded young nettles are an effective natural accelerator.
Your compost pile is too wet, too slimy or too soggy?	Add dry materials such as hay and straw, autumn leaves, shredded paper or torn-up cardboard, sawdust and other "browns". A handful of material in your compost should not clump together when squeezed in your fist.
The compost heap is too slimy. Layers are matted and clumped in places.	If you have too much of any one material in your compost, it will tend to have slimy layers. When you layer grass trimmings or clippings too thickly and you don't

	aerate well, you'll see slimy matting as a result. Break up the slimy layer and incorporate straw, dry leaves, crunched up paper or wood shavings. Turn the heap regularly to get more air in. A cold heap is still decomposing although it will take longer to mature.
Raccoons are scavenging in your compost heap.	Hinge a wooden or metal lid to your compost bin, or if your heap is on the ground, enclose it with wire mesh. Bar the raccoons from entry to your compost. You might not wish to trap or poison them as they probably are just too hungry or too curious to leave your pile alone!
Your compost heap is "too cold". It is damp and sweet-smelling but it doesn't heat up.	Heat up your compost pile by adding "activators" such as well-rotted chicken dung, comfrey leaves, young weeds, grass and hedge trimmings, kitchen scraps and other nitrogen-rich materials. You can also put in a

	limited amount of fresh livestock manure.
The compost is damp and warm in the middle but elsewhere it is dry.	Increase the size of your compost heap. Put in more materials - both greens and browns. Moisten the mix evenly and turn to incorporate air.
The compost heap is steaming.	A hot and steamy pile is not a problem. It simply means that a battalion of microscopic critters are hard at work, decomposing your compost.
Weeds are sprouting all over your compost. You suspect that there are more weed seeds in your heap.	Turn the heap to mix in the sprouting weeds. Weed seeds may survive in compost when the mix is not hot enough. Eliminate the seeds before they germinate in your garden. You know that your compost is hot enough when, as you dip your hand into the heap, it's too hot for comfort! Ideally, for weed seeds to die, the inside of the heap should be 130^0F to 150^0F (54.4^0C to 65.6^0C) for at least one month. Turn over the heap and mix up the compost

	regularly to equalize the heating. A compost tumbler is great for this job. Weed-free straw used for animal bedding is a good bulking material for your compost.

HOW CAN YOU MAKE YOUR OWN COMPOST?

By making your own compost you help nature rebuild its basic growth medium - the soil. Composting "is the perfect lazy person's gardening project. Unlike weeding or double-digging, which take lots of time and physical effort, a compost pile pretty much takes care of itself. Build it right, and it will transform your growing expectations". (planetnatural.com)

The magic of organic waste recycling - participate in it by making your own compost at home. With virtually no expense and little effort, you can mimic nature's humus-making process. Enthusiasts and experts conclude that it's hard to mess up compost, but the beginner could use an ample dose of tips and techniques to get off to a good start.

Seven steps to making your own compost, the open-heap way.

1. Bare earth is the first essential of open-heap or traditional composting.
 There might already be resident wigglers and other microorganisms in this bare patch of earth. Choose a "sunny yet shady" corner of your backyard or available space. The sun's heat will help maintain the temperature your microbes are happy to live in. The site needs to have some shade also because too much direct exposure to the sun can dry your compost to a crisp, especially if water is scarce or the beginner's enthusiasm flags along the way. When the compost heap is in a very shady corner, decomposition, especially during the freezing temps, is much slower.

2. Spread a mixed layer of twigs or straw first - up to half a foot deep. This porous layer facilitates drainage and allows air to flow within the pile.

3. Put in roughly equal amounts of the greens and browns in alternate layers.

The greens, at this step should be mainly kitchen scraps. You can also loosely mix them up instead of neatly layering them. Too much of the moist materials in one place will make them clump together. Too much of the dry materials will have too little nutrients for the microbes to feed on. Don't be too worried of getting the browns to greens ratio perfect - just observe that they are evenly layered or nicely mixed together.

4. Now you can add microbe-rich animal manure to activate the composting process. If you don't wish to include this yucky stuff in your compost heap, you can stick to "green manure". Green manure are nitrogen-rich plant parts such as hedge or shrubbery trimmings, grass clippings, clover, wheatgrass, buckwheat or any other discarded plant matter, including shredded weeds and leaves.

5. Keep your compost heap moist but not too wet. Water your compost occasionally and more frequently during the dry months as evaporation tends to dry the mix. It is better to use the fine spray nozzle of a garden hose than drenching the mound by the pitchers-full. If heavy rain makes the pile soggy, loosen it a bit with a pitchfork to break up matted or compacted sections.

6. Cover your compost mound. Spread a few inches of coarse sawdust or wood shavings. You may use carpet scraps, plastic sheeting, heavy burlap or any other appropriate material. You cover the compost heap so you retain moisture and maintain heat. The beneficial microbes thrive in a damp, moist and warm environment. It is necessary to cover your pile in winter or seasons of heavy rainfall. If you can't keep the compost covered, rearrange the mound in such a way that excess water drains off instead of it seeping into and soaking the mix.

7. Turn your compost at least once every two weeks. With a shovel or pitchfork, turn over the contents of the heap. This allows air to freely move in the heap - and the busy microbes get fresh supplies of oxygen. If the occasional turning proves

too taxing, you can put in more coarse material like dry leaves and straw. You can also put in several branchy stakes to hold up the mixed materials so these don't get compacted, especially in winter or rainy season. By mixing and turning the compost, you can also check for the presence of vermin and rodents who find the pile too comfy to pass up. (eartheasy.com)

Seven steps to making your own compost, the containerized way:

1. Find the right container and put it in the right site.
Choose from a wide variety of manufactured compost bins available from gardening centers and hardware stores. Access their sites and decide on the bin that suits your home. There are bins suited to be in the backyard and there are bins appropriate in size and features to be kept in your garage or even in your kitchen. If you put your bin in the backyard, mount it over bare earth in a "sunny but shady" location - not too hot for contents to broil nor too cold for the compost mix to languish. Ensure you provide for the leachate to be captured if you place your bin over tarmac, paving or patio slabs to avoid staining. Also, think ahead to the time you would harvest the end-product. Check that you can easily add ingredients and crank the bin if it is not an automatic drum tumbler.

2. Put in the right ingredients.
Collect your food scraps into a handy kitchen caddy or simply use an old ice cream tub, plastic canister or stainless-steel bucket with lid. Regular tin containers tend to rust. Keep these containers covered because fruit flies have very sensitive smell mechanisms. You won't welcome swarms of these tiny flies, or worse, the aggressive houseflies to invade your kitchen.
Fruit and vegetable peelings, teabags, torn up cereal boxes, toilet roll tubes and eggshells can all go into your caddy. If your compost bin has a secure lid, you can include out-of-date food, scraps of cooked food and leftovers. Meat, fish, bones,

entrails and offals are best pre-cooked before adding into anaerobic digesters such as bokashi bins and other specially-designed organic waste converter bins. If you choose to put these animal products in the outdoor bins, bury them deep into the mix.

3. Fill up your compost bin.
You don't have to wait for your kitchen caddy to reach full capacity. Toss the contents into your compost bin along with other garden waste. The perfect no-hassle-recipe for good compost is a rough 50/50 mix of browns and greens. See that the dry and tougher carbon-rich materials like newspapers and cardboard are torn up or shredded to hasten breakdown by microbes.

4. Now it's time to wait and it might take a while.
In containerized composting, the compost could take up to one year to mature. Nature is doing its work while you wait. Meanwhile, it is a good idea to have two or three compost bins so you can have compost at varying stages of decomposition. Add the browns and the greens to the tops of the compost mix while leaving the bottom mix to continue decomposing. In rotating compost bins, the old and the new materials get mixed up. The new waste provide fresh food for the microbes while the old material generate heat to hasten the breaking down of the new mix.

5. Your compost is ready for use.
After what can seem to be forever, your compost is finally ready to use. The gardener's gold resembles moist and crumbly dark soil - your own mimicked humus. By now the smell receptors in your nose have been sensitized enough to appreciate the fresh earthy aroma of compost.

6. Remove your compost from the bin.
If your compost bin is not a drum tumbler, you need to lift and tilt it slightly to empty the contents. (Careful about your back when you lift!) Some bins have bottoms that open for easier harvesting. Whichever type of compost bin you used, the task

now is to scoop out the finished compost with a spade, garden fork or trowel. Time to celebrate your composting beginner's luck? Pat yourself on the back - all your effort is worth it: you have done your little bit to improve the ecosystem.

7. **Use your compost.**
It is perfectly normal to have bits of eggshell, un-decomposed hard bits of kitchen scraps such as nutshells and bones, and little lumps of twigs in your finished compost. You can toss these back into the old pile to start a fresh heap. Use the product of your labor to enrich your vegetable patch and flower gardens, freshen up your ornamentals in the patio containers or "top-dress" your lawn. (recyclenow.com)

HOW YOU CAN USE YOUR COMPOST?

How can you tell if your compost is ready?
Now that you have succeeded to turn out good compost (or at least a respectable semblance of the real thing), you can use it in a variety of ways in your garden. Is your compost ready? Good quality compost is dark like the soil you find on the forest floor. From the time you start to when you are ready to use it, compost takes between four months and two years.

As a beginner, you might occasionally neglect your compost heap or you don't quite get the browns to greens ratio right, or your pile may be a little too big or too small. Don't worry - compost piles, like Mother Nature, are generally forgiving. Like magic, the composted materials will all eventually break down. Your first compost may not look like the packaged compost sold at the garden centres or shops. Yours may have bits of eggshell, twigs and lumps of other stuff in it - but it's still perfect for your garden. Simply put back the larger bits and lumps back into your heap or compost bin.

The "finished" compost is dark brown, loose and crumbly, moist and smells like fresh earth. Some clumps of un-decomposed material may be there. You can sift these out with a metal screen or you can just rake them up and put into a new compost heap. You can leave the old pile to finish decomposing instead of adding new materials to it. As with any new skill, you will learn more of home composting by actually getting your hands messy.

As you add water to your compost in the bin, some of the nutrients will filter down to the soil beneath. Place your bin strategically - on a spot you plan to turn into a flowerbed or vegetable plot or where you plan to plant a fruit or ornamental tree. The leachate from your compost will enrich that spot.You can move your compost bin each time the compost has matured, leaving behind enriched soil that you can simply dig up a little and you can put in your new plants.

Adding or incorporating compost into hard, compacted or clayey soils makes them more porous for beneficial microorganisms to thrive, suppressing some plant diseases. Compost helps to keep the pH balance of your garden soil in check as well as maintain the moisture levels. Compost can neutralize very acidic or very alkaline soils to better suit them for particular crops. Fresh compost provides everything your plants need such as potassium, nitrogen and phosphorus.

Use your compost only as an additive to the garden soil. Pure compost is too rich to be used as the sole growing medium for your plants. The rich organic matter in compost provides a lot of nutrients for growing plants but, like a concentrate human diet that needs to be diluted, compost needs to be spread in a garden bed for the nutrients to be efficiently utilized. There are so many places you can use your homemade compost.

Grow healthier vegetables and herbs

Garden vegetables will grow robustly when compost is added to the soil. Tuber veggies like carrots and potatoes would do exceptionally well when the soil is porous. In hard or compacted soils, carrots tend to "branch". Compost will intensify the natural colors of your vegetables: the greens more vibrant, the yellows more radiant, the reds more intense and all the varied colors luxuriant. Parsley, chives, mint, coriander and other aromatics will flourish in your herb garden with the addition of compost.

Compost will nourish your flowerbeds and other plants

Before you put in your flower seedlings, incorporate compost into the soil. When directly planting very tiny flower seeds, you can mix very fine compost or sand with the seeds. This way, it is easier to spread the seeds out evenly in the garden bed. If you already have the flowers or other plants in the bed, just add the compost-enriched soil around the base of the plants - taking care that soft stems are not in direct contact with the compost. As you water the flowers and other plants, the nutrients will trickle down to the roots.

Feed your fruit trees and ornamental shrubs

Orchard keepers recognize the value of compost. Fruit trees need nutrients at different stages of development. When farmers set out the saplings, they normally dig holes deep enough to at least half the height of the baby trees. A mixture of orchard soil and compost is poured into the holes and watered generously. The samplings are then carefully planted into the holes. The trees are continuously nurtured to the budding, fruiting and harvesting stages. Fruit farmers prefer compost over chemical fertilizers, especially if their orchards are several hundreds of acres big. Compost protects trees against some diseases, partly because of the microbes still fighting off harmful and invasive bacteria and fungi. Compost at the base of trees controls weed growth and keeps in moisture to tide the trees over prolonged drought.

Use compost to enrich the new plots and borders

When you expand your garden plots or break new ground for more crops, the soil may not be ready for planting. Mixing compost into the soil insures new colonies of beneficial microorganisms that get down to work immediately. Distribute an even layer of compost over the newly dug plots. Work the compost into the soil, add earthworms if you can buy some from worm breeders. These efficient critters will further mix in the compost for you, ensuring that your plants will utilize the nutrients better. Earthworms are also great natural aerators of the soil as they tunnel through their underground domain. Remember to leave a gap between the soft stems of new seedlings when you apply fresh compost to prevent scorching.

Nourish your lawn

Sieve your compost first before you apply it to your lawn to separate larger bits of material such as twigs and scraps that have not quite decomposed yet. Check that the lawn grass is mature because fresh compost can be too hot for newly seeded lawns. The roots of newly laid-out turf need to get established. Add an equal amount of sharp sand to your sifted compost. Adding sand or similar loose soil to the compost will make spreading easier. Apply a thin and even layer, less than three centimeters thick. For new lawns or young grass, use compost more sparingly so they don't get scorched by the strength of the rich ingredients.

Use compost as mulch.

A 3-inch layer of rough compost around shrubs and over flowerbeds controls erosion while replenishing the soil. Everything in the compost mix that has not completely broken down serves as good mulch. Gardeners, anticipating the onset of heavy rains, add compost mulch on the soils to prevent erosion and to shield them from the full force of the elements. Newly seeded plots are also mulched to protect the sprouting plants from scorching heat and pounding raindrops.

Re-invigorate your potted plants

Repeated waterings of your potted plants can compact and wash down some of the nutrients in the potting soil. Replenish these nutrients by mixing in compost to the top few inches of the soil in the pots. If your plants are soft-stemmed, leave a gap between the stems and the compost, just to make sure the stems don't get burned. Some of your potted plants may have outlived their containers. Gently remove them and loosen the compacted soil. You may find that the roots have gotten all tangled and cramped. Mix compost with fresh potting soil and put back your plants into the pots. You may wish to split the old plants into several pots to give them a fresh environment to expand and bloom. Weed and grass seeds may be in the compost. When these sprout, pull them out and leave them to dry as "mulch" or simply dig them into the potting soil.

HEALTH HAZARDS AND RISKS OF COMPOSTING

Processing household organic waste is profitable at the beginner's level. The "profits" may not readily translate into cash, but the satisfaction of feeding plants and seeing the luxuriant growth is reward enough. Commercial composting is big business, driven by the outcry from environmentalists demanding accountability over ecological integrity. Composting provides employment and related livelihoods. Whether you are a beginner or already making a good living out of composting, you need to be aware of the potential health hazards and risks of the venture.

The shredding and periodic turning of compost can expose workers to harmful bioaerosols. Bioaerosols are very tiny airborne particles originating from biological substances. These very fine dust-like particles get separated from the larger materials when such are stirred or handled or transported by water, air and wind. Bioaerosols containing fungal spores and harmful bacteria are ubiquitous - they are just about everywhere.

Some people, especially those with allergies, react to bioaerosols. Foster (2012) cited some incidences in work sites where airborne pathogens caused mild to severe reactions such as nausea, headaches, fatigue and breathing problems. People with weak immune systems can be particularly susceptible to bioaerosol infections. (scotsman.com)

Harmful organisms thrive in decaying organic matter such as compost. Most of these die off during the heating and curing compost process. Compost laid out in the open emit more of these particles than the compost in closed containers. Composters take health measures to prevent the damaging effects of bioaerosols. Healthy people are able to bear exposure to bioaerosols without any ill effects. Gromiko (nachi.org) offers the following helpful information on composting hazards.

Diseases contracted from handling compost:

Dangerous pathogens can breed in compost and unsuspecting gardeners could get very ill or even killed by prolonged exposure. A few of the common ailments that afflict unprotected compost workers are the following:

Aspergillosis, a fungal lung infection, normally not life-threatening, can be fatally dangerous. Gardeners, engulfed in clouds of compost dust, may inhale fungus spores.

Pneumonia-like **Farmer's Lung** affects workers who handle rotting organic materials like hay, sugar cane and mushrooms. Dusty white patches on plants are danger signs.

Histoplasmosis is another respiratory infection caused by the fungus thriving on bird droppings and guano (bat poop). Most lung infections are treated with antibiotics. As a precautionary measure, those who handle soil and compost should get their tetanus shots. Long exposure to moisture and minor cuts and abrasions can allow any number of bacteria to enter the body.

Paronychia is a painful infection affecting the skin surrounding fingernails and toenails.

Potential hazards of composting could be avoided

Dangerous fungi and bacteria can thrive in compost and garden soil. Those who expose themselves to potential harmful pathogens should heed safety precautions. Wear closed-toed footwear so your feet will not be in direct contact with compost and always leave the footwear outdoors. When you use gardening tools, wear dry and "breathable" gloves - not those that cause your hands to perspire. Always wear a dust mask, nose and mouth guard or any protective swathing when you stir and till the compost. If possible, don't till or stir compost on windy days. Airtight or fully-closed containers are not recommended for compost storage - without any air, the contents can readily catch fire. Garden enthusiasts can get so absorbed in their tasks that they could overlook some obvious safety and hygiene measures. Never fail to thoroughly wash your hands after handling compost. Seek medical attention as soon as you observe any skin infection or when you develop a severe cough after getting exposed to compost or garden work.

Compost fires

While "self-incinerating" compost fires can be extremely rare, they nonetheless occur. A great deal of heat is generated by microbial activity in compost heaps and occasionally, it is enough to ignite a fire. In addition to the biological heating, airflow could be limited in bulky well-insulated piles. Neglect or oversight could result in dry pockets of materials within the heap, non-uniform mixing of materials and unevenly distributed moisture may subject compost heaps to combustion. Electrical mishaps, lit cigarettes, insufficiently cooled ash added to the heap are common causes of compost fires. You can prevent your compost heap from catching fire by heeding these tips. Check that your compost is properly aerated. Ventilate the heap by turning it yourself or by using a mechanical aerator, as in a tumbler bin. Compost in containers can also overheat and generate high levels of methane, a flammable gas. Rotate the bin daily.

Monitor the temperature of your compost heap with a long thermometer that can reach the core. If the reading goes beyond 160°F (71.10C), your pile is too hot. Make your heap smaller (divide a huge pile into two smaller heaps). Re-mix the contents, adding coarse and bulky material such as wood chips and shredded dry leaves or straw. Evenly spray water as you turn the pile. If, unfortunately your compost does catch fire, wait until the fire has completely died out before you attempt to turn the heap (or whatever is left of it). The rush of oxygen to a turned smoldering heap can make your pile erupt into flames. Of course, this is a tip for dummies: avoid heaping compost next to flammable structures!

Compost-friendly pests

Compost heaps attract a host of unwelcome pests - flies, beetles, termites, cockroaches - to name just a few. And where the prey is, the predator surely follows. Mice and rats go after these pests (and also to feast on the food scraps). The house cat is on the prowl too. Portable composters with lids can keep most of the scavengers away. If your compost heap is out in the open, try burying all the tempting morsels deep inside. Keep your piles "vegetarian" if possible - leave bones, meat, cheese, eggs and fats in the covered compost bins. Also, be considerate of the neighbors - some compost piles can be fetid, even after you take careful measures to contain the foul smells.

All in all, Gromiko (nachi.org) concludes: "the benefits of compost piles can be quickly eclipsed by health hazards and nuisances if they are not designed correctly and maintained properly".

CONCLUSION

As a beginner in composting, you might be intimidated and bewildered by all the "how to" tips and techniques. Take it easy - don't get overwhelmed. Composting, at its simplest and "fun-nest" form, is not rocket science. You can do it and even if your first attempts don't earn you a A+, just relish the experience. Compost will not hold a grudge against you even if you don't get the ratios right. Jump in and try any of the composting techniques you've read about. You'll find out for yourself what works and what needs more tweaking. Making good compost has no hidden mystery.

Your compost heap simply mimics the way nature recycles organic matter. Experiment different mixes and use a variety of techniques. You'll get the hang of it after a while. Get smart about using your food scraps and plant trimmings - feed the earth and replenish its reserves. The satisfaction you get from your happy plants will more than compensate for the many hours you tinker and putter around in the garden.

REFERENCES

Dougherty, Mark. Field Guide to On-Farm Composting. Ithaca, New York: Natural Resource   Agriculture, and Engineering Service. 1999.

Edmonton composting facility

Hemenway, Toby (2009). Gaia's Garden: A Guide to Home-Scale Permaculture. Chelsea Green Publishing. pp. 84-85. ISBN 978-1-60358-029-8.

"hugelkultur: the ultimate raised garden beds". Richsoil.com. 2007-07-27. Retrieved 2013-07-18.

Jenkins, J.C. (2005). The Humanure Handbook: A Guide to Composting Human Manure. Grove City, PA: Joseph Jenkins, Inc.; 3rd edition. p. 255. ISBN 978-0-9644258-3-5. Retrieved April 2011.

Lazcano, Cristina; Gómez-Brandón, María; Domínguez, Jorge (2008). "Comparison of the effectiveness of composting and vermicomposting for the biological stabilization of cattle manure". Chemosphere 72: 1013–1019. doi:10.1016/j.chemosphere.2008.04.016.

Lindsay, Jay "Japanese composting may be new food waste solution". AP. 12 June 2012. Retrieved 13 November 2012.

"Paper on Invasive European Worms". Retrieved 22 February 2009.

Symons, Courtney. "'Humanure' dumping sickens homeowner". YourOttawaRegion. Metroland Media Group Ltd. 13 October 2011. Retrieved 16 October 2011.

Winker, Martina . Pharmaceutical residures in urine and potential risks related to use as fertilzer in agriculture. Doctoral dissertation, 2009

Sources retrieved from the web:

http://www.cleanup.org.au/au/LivingGreener/composting.html

http://www.epa.gov/compost/types.htm

http://www2.epa.gov/recycle/composting-home

http://www.epa.gov/waste/conserve/foodwaste/

http://www.excelind.co.in/Excel_ENBT/wasteTreatment.html

http://www.nachi.org/compost-pile-hazards.htm compost hazards. Gromiko, Nick.

http://www.recyclenow.com/reduce/home-composting

http://www.recyclenow.com/reduce/home-composting/faqs/making-compost-faqs

http://www.recyclenow.com/reduce/home-composting/making-compost/composting-easy-step-step-guide

http://www.recyclenow.com/reduce/home-composting/using-your-compost

http://www.scotsman.com/news/environment/concerns-over-composting-as-study-reveals-health-risks-of-recycling-organic-household-waste-1-2248755 by Foster, Kate. Published on 22 April 2012.

http://www.thewormdude.com/products-page/the-bio-pod-plus-and-black-soldier-fly-larvae

Sources not cited in the book, but nonetheless, consulted for information:

http://www.bbc.co.uk/gardening/basics/techniques/soil_makecompost1.shtml

http://www.planetnatural.com/composting-101/

http://www.organicgardening.com/learn-and-grow/composting-101

http://www.calrecycle.ca.gov/organics/homecompost/

http://home.howstuffworks.com/composting.htm

http://www.canadiangardening.com/how-to/techniques/compost-basics/a/1488

http://www.compostguy.com/composting-basics/

http://cleantechnica.com/2009/03/03/bokashi-this-is-not-your-fathers-compost/

http://www.greencalgary.org/resources/bokashi-composting/

http://www.gardenguides.com/123125-outside-gourmet-compost-bin-instructions.html

http://www.hse.gov.uk/waste/composting.htm

http://permaculturenews.org/2010/08/03/the-art-and-science-of-making-a-hugelkultur-bed-transforming-woody-debris-into-a-garden-resource/

If you enjoyed this book, I would appreciate if you could leave an Amazon review as that would greatly help self-published authors like myself. Thank you!

Made in the USA
San Bernardino, CA
03 March 2020